NATIONAL SECURITY AGENCY
Ft. George G. Meade, MD

I0410921

Serial: I732-010R-2008
30 April 2008

Network Infrastructure Division
Systems and Network Analysis Center

<u>Activating Authentication and Encryption</u>
<u>for Cisco CallManager 4.(x)</u>

Table of Contents

1.0 Executive Summary

The intent of this document is to provide step by step instructions for configuring authentication and encryption for Cisco CallManager (CCM) releases 4.0(x) through 4.3(x) and the supported Cisco IP phones. Although, Cisco has a very comprehensive document covering this topic, it is hard to follow and some steps are not in the right order. This document is a 'Cliff Notes" version of Cisco's security guide. The document will provide high level system requirements, restrictions, instructions for loading and configuring the Certificate Trust List (CTL), Certificate Authority Proxy Function (CAPF) Service, phone security mode, and hardening the phone.

2.0 Introduction and Security Overview

When Voice over Internet Protocol (VoIP) users are asked about security concerns related to VoIP, one of the first thoughts was how to secure the VoIP network itself. Although, applying security measures at Layer 2 through Layer 5 (switches, routers, firewalls, and IDS) are important and necessary, it does not fully encompass Defense in Depth strategy. To take full advantage of Defense in Depth countermeasures, the presentation layer (Layer 6) must also be implemented to encrypt the media.

To set a base line for understanding authentication and encryption, basic terminologies need to be understood. This section will provide an understanding of why authentication and encryption is important. The terminologies used throughout the document will be defined in Table 1 below. The use of authentication and encryption will protect confidentiality and make it harder for individuals (internal and external) from tampering with the signaling and media streams, the CCM server, and IP phones. To be compliant with Information Assurance Directorate's (IAD) guidance, authentication and encryption services must be activated on CCM and the associated Cisco IP phones on the network. When the security features are activated, the media streams and call signaling between Cisco IP phones are encrypted, the files sent between the CCM and the phones are digitally signed, and the network communication streams are authenticated.

Table 1. Definition of terminologies extracted from Cisco documentation.

Term	Definition
Authentication	Process that verifies the identity of an entity.
Advanced Encrypted Standard (AES)	AES is a symmetric key encryption algorithm and is adopted by the U.S. Government, Department of Defense, and private industry world wide for data encryption.
Certificate Authority Proxy Function (CAPF)	Process whereby supported devices can request locally significant certificates by using Cisco CallManager Administration.
Certificate Trust List (CTL)	List that Cisco IP Phones use; a file that you create after you install and configure the Cisco CTL client in the Cisco CallManager cluster; contains a predefined list of trusted items

	that the Cisco Site Administrator eToken (security token) signs; provides authentication information to validate the certificates for servers and eTokens for Cisco IP Phones.
Administrator Security Token (security token: etoken)	A portable hardware security module that contains a private key and an X.509v3 certificate that the Cisco Certificate Authority signs; used for file authentication, it signs the CTL file and retrieves the private key of the certificate. In some Cisco's documents, the Site Administrator Security Token (SAST) is the same as the Cisco security e-Token.
Device Authentication	Process that validates the identity of the device and ensures that the entity is what it claims to be.
Encryption	Process that ensures that only the intended recipient receives and reads the data; process that ensures the confidentiality of the information; process that translates data into cipher text, which appears random and meaningless.
File Authentication	Process that validates digitally signed files that the phone downloads. The phone validates the signature to make sure that file tampering did not occur after the file creation.
Hypertext Transfer Protocol over Secure Sockets Layer (HTTPS)	An IETF-defined protocol that ensures (at a minimum) the identity of the HTTPS server; by using encryption, ensures the confidentiality of the information that is exchanged between the IIS server and the browser client.
Image Authentication	Process that prevents tampering with the binary image prior to loading it on the phone; process whereby a phone validates the integrity and source of an image.
Integrity	Process that ensures that data tampering has not occurred between entities.
Locally Significant Certification (LSC)	A digital x.509v3 certificate that is installed on the phone; issued by a third-party certificate authority CAPF.
Media Encryption	Process whereby the confidentiality of the media occurs by using cryptographic procedures. Media encryption uses Secure Real Time Protocol (SRTP) as defined in IETF RFC 3711.
Manufacture Installed Certificate (MIC)	A digital x.509v3 certificate that is signed by the Cisco Certificate authority and installed in supported phones by Cisco Manufacturing.
Mixed Mode	Mode within a cluster that you configured for security; includes authenticated and non-authenticated devices that connect to the Cisco CallManager.
Non-secure Call	Call in which at least one device is not authenticated or encrypted.
Secure Call	Call in which all devices are authenticated, and the media stream is encrypted.
Signaling Authentication	Process that validates that no tampering occurred to signaling packets during transmission; uses the Transport Layer Security protocol.

Signaling Encryption	Process that uses cryptographic methods to protect the confidentiality of all SCCP signaling messages that are sent between the device and the Cisco CallManager server.
Trivial File Transfer Protocol (TFTP)	TFTP is a simple file transfer protocol used by the phones to get its setting from the CCM server or TFTP server.
Transport Layer Security (TLS)	A security protocol that IETF defines and that provides integrity, authentication, and encryption and resides in the TCP layer in the IP communications stack.

3.0   System Requirements and Restrictions

In order to activate the authentication and encryption on CCM 4.(x), the following system requirements and restrictions must be considered:

Requirements:

- Cisco provided operating system Windows 2000 Advanced Server version 2000.2.6 or later.
- Service Pack 3a for Windows 2000 Advanced Server or later.
- All Cisco CCM servers in the cluster must be on 4.0(x).
- Minimum of two Cisco security eTokens or SAST for Certificate Trust List (CTL) client.

Restrictions and Interactions:

- Media and signaling encryption will not work if the Cisco CTL client service is not activated and installed throughout all the CCM servers (publisher and subscribers) in the same cluster.
- Auto-registration does not work in a cluster with mixed mode, which is required for device authentication.
- During an encrypted call, a non-encrypted Cisco 7970 IP phone user cannot barge into an existing encrypted call. To do so, the 7970 used for barging must be configured to support encryption.
- When Cisco 7960 and Cisco 7940 IP phones are provisioned with encryption in the cluster, those phones cannot accept a barge request while taking part on the call.
- CCM only supports authenticated and encrypted calls between secure Cisco IP phones within a single cluster. CCM does not support the security features when calls are made outside of the cluster and to other end-points using Session Initiation Protocol (SIP), H.323 protocol, ad hoc conferences, music on hold, and Media Gateway Control Protocol (MGCP).

Notes: Listed above are primary restrictions, interactions, and requirements. Detailed listing of all requirements, restrictions, and interactions, refers to Chapter 1 of the Cisco CallManager Security Guide at:
http://www.cisco.com/en/US/docs/voice_ip_comm/cucm/security/4_1_2/secugd.pdf.

It is highly recommended that the administrators review the best practices provided by Cisco prior to activating authentication and encryption on the CCM and Cisco IP phones. These best practices include backing up the system, restoring data using the Backup and Restore System (BARS) utility, and activating security options during maintenance hours. This information is available in Chapter 1 of the above link.

4.0 Configuring Security

4.1 Activating Certificate Trust List (CTL) and Certificate Authority Proxy Function (CAPF) Service

The CTL service must be activated and configured manually on a single Windows 2000 workstation (could be the CCM publisher). It is also necessary to activate the CTL service on all the other servers (subscribers) in the same cluster. The CCM publisher will not push the service activation to other servers in the cluster. The CAPF service is activated only on the CCM publisher database server.

Note: The IP addresses and server name utilized in the following examples are fictitious information. Insert the appropriate network information for your network.

To activate CTL Client and CAPF services, go to Cisco CallManager Administrator and follow these steps:

Step 1. Select **Application → Cisco CallManager Serviceability → Tools → Service Activation**.

Cisco Unified CallManager 4.2 Administration

Details

Copyright © 1999 - 2004 Cisco Systems, Inc.
All rights reserved.

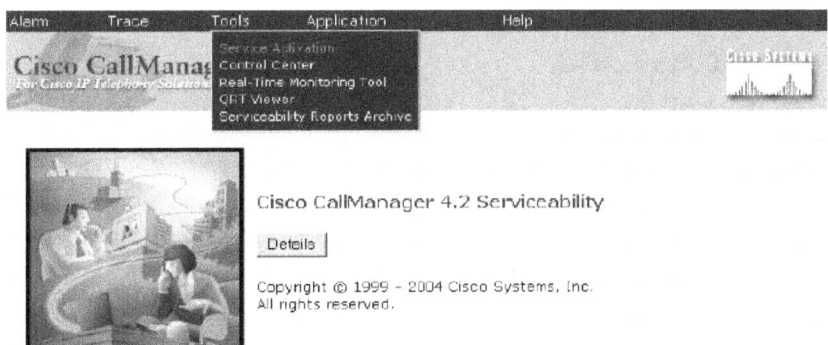

Step 2. Find your CCM server in the cluster and open the service activation screen (upper left corner of the screen).

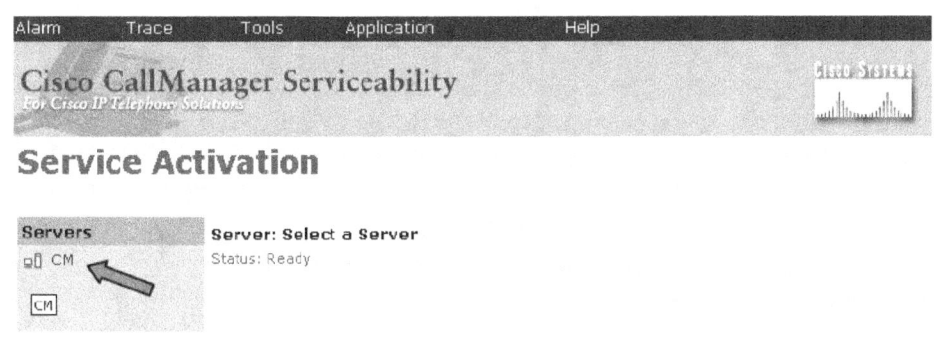

Step 3. Look under the NT Service section and place a check in the **Cisco CTL Provider** and **Cisco Certificate Authority Proxy Function** to activate the two services.

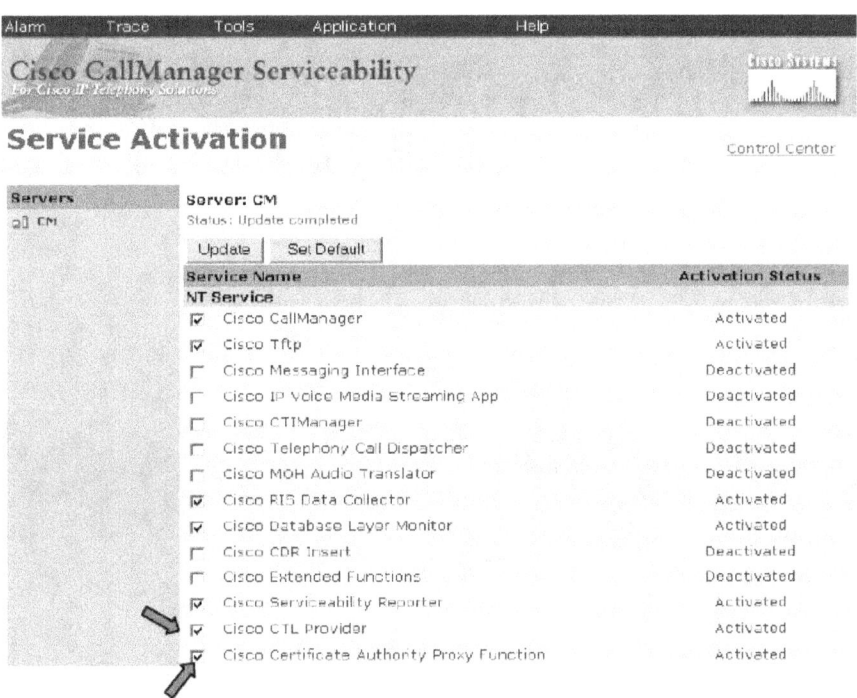

Step 4. Click **Update.**

Step 5. Confirm the service activation by going to **Application** → **Cisco CallManager Serviceability** → **Tools** → **Control Center.**

Cisco CAPF service parameters are set with default values. To change the default values, proceed with the following steps:

Step 6. In Cisco CallManager Administration, choose **Service** → **Service Parameters.**

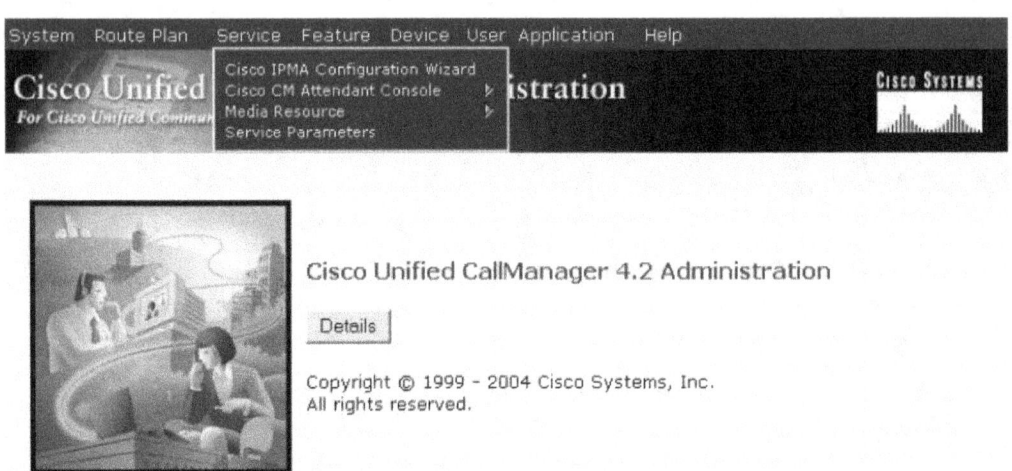

Step 7. From the drop-down Server and Service boxes, select your CCM and the **Cisco Certificate Authority Proxy Function.**

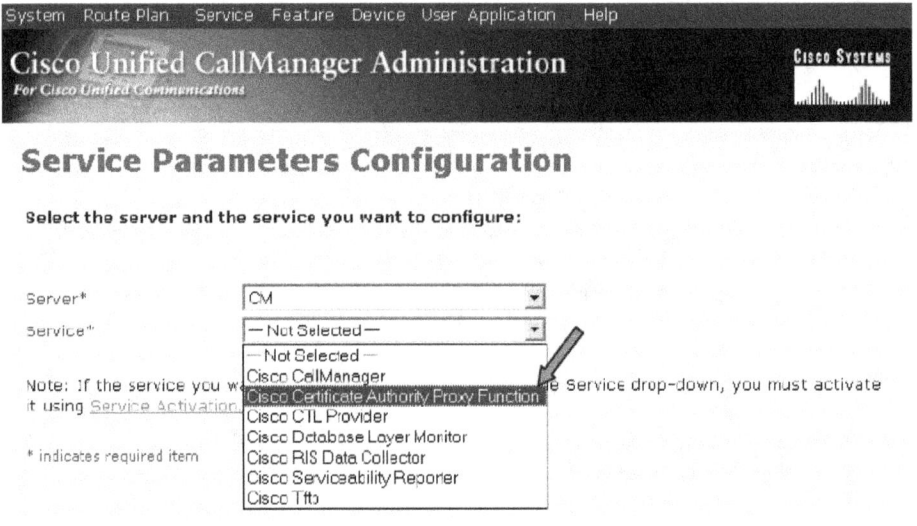

Step 8. Accept the default values or modify them accordingly. Click on the blue "i" icon on the upper right hand corner for the description of the fields.

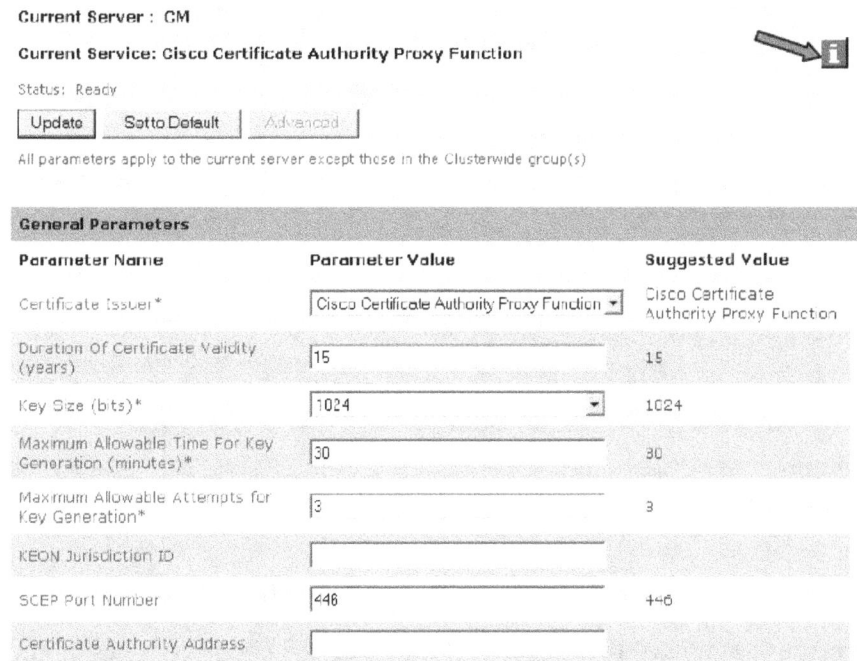

Step 9. Click **Update** and restart the CAPF service if changes were made to the default values.

Step 10. To change default value for **Cisco CTL Provider** TLS connection port, repeat *Step 6* and this time select **Cisco CTL Provider** instead of CAPF.

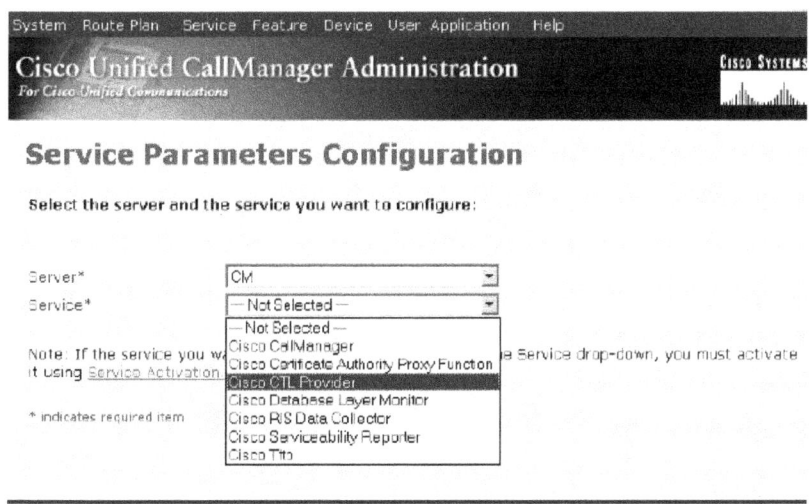

Step 11. Click **Update** and restart the CTL Provider service if change was made to the default value.

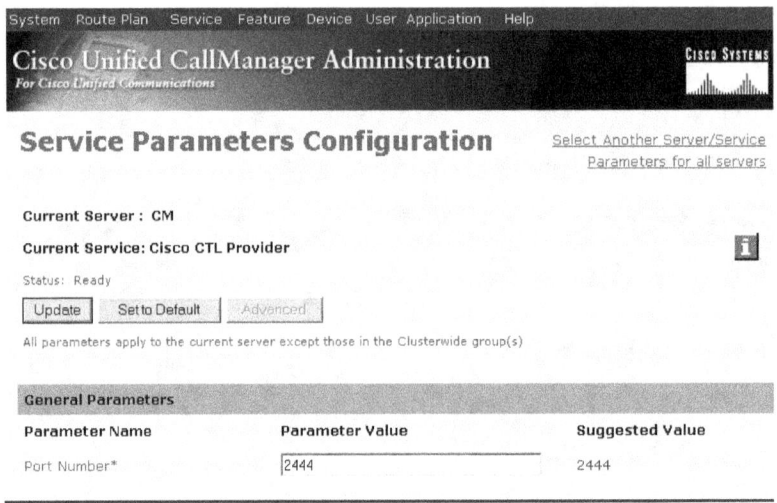

4.2   *Installing and Configuring the Cisco Certificate Trust List*

Now that you have activated the Cisco CTL Provider and CAPF services on the Window 2000 workstation, your next step is to install the Cisco CTL Provider on that same workstation. Before you can install the Cisco CTL Provider, you must make sure that the Smart Card Service is set to start automatically on the Windows 2000 server. If this service is not activated, the installation of the Cisco CTL Provider will fail.

These items and information will be required in order to complete the process:

- Have at least two Cisco security eTokens.
- The security eTokens administrative passwords (see page 15, *step 18* for default password).
- The CCM IP address.
- The Username and Password to your CCM.

Step 1. On the Windows server where your CCM is located, choose **Start → Programs → Administrative Tools → Services**.

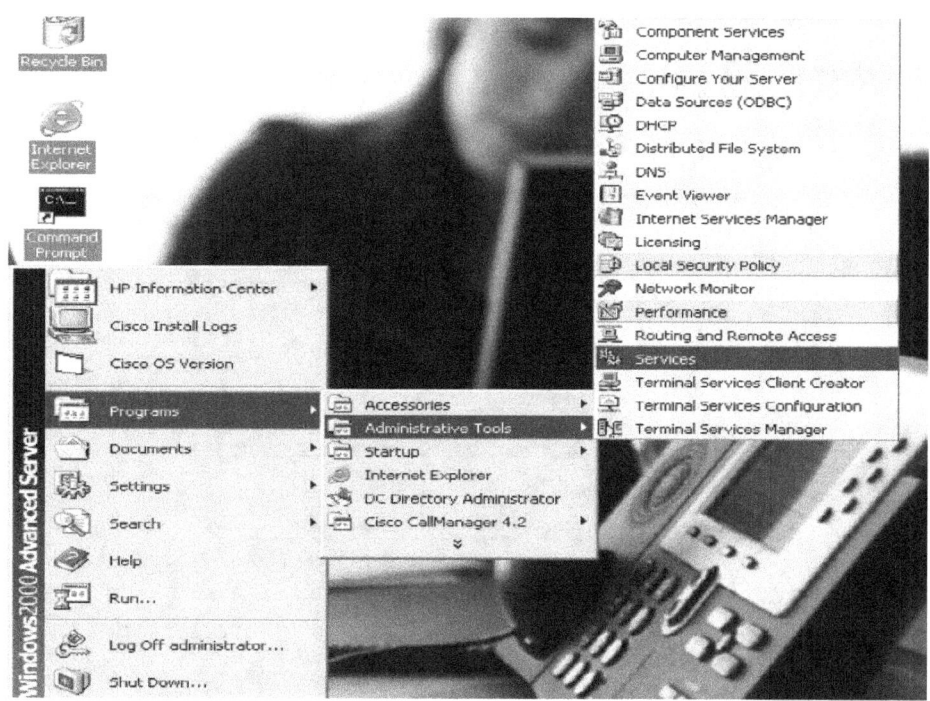

Step 2. Find **Smart Card** and double-click on the service.

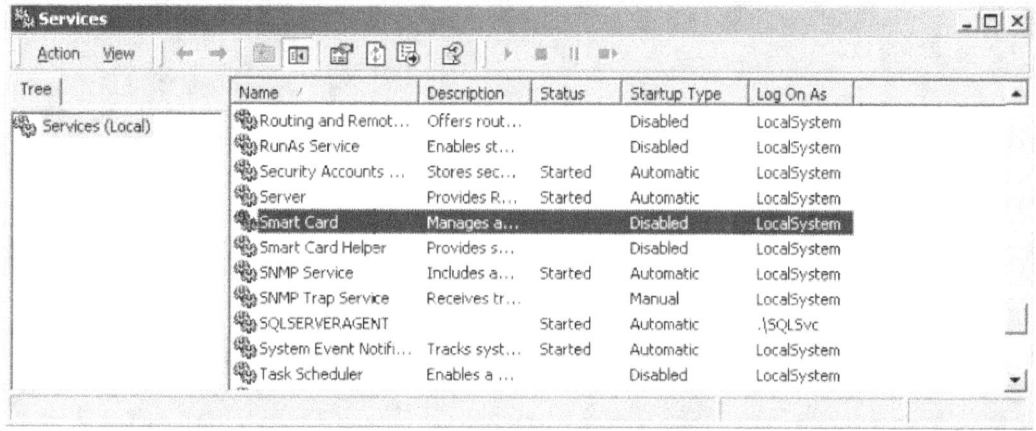

Step 3. Click on the Startup type drop down menu and set it to **Automatic**.

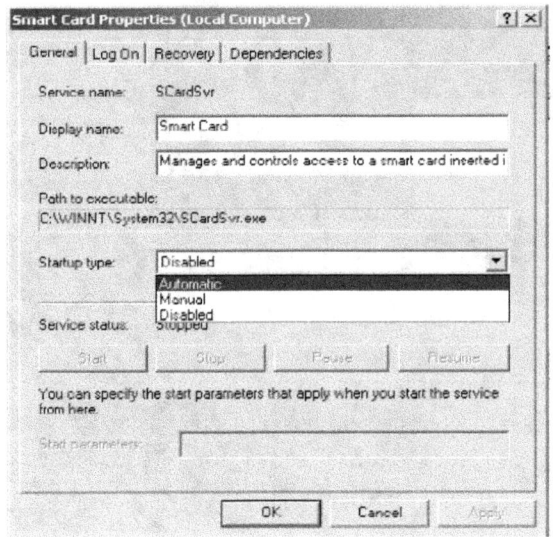

Step 4. Click **Apply.**

Step 5. Click **Start.**

Step 6. Click **OK.**

The next step in the process is to install the CTL Client plug-in. From Cisco CallManager Administration:

Step 7. Click on **Application → Install Plugins**.

Step 8. Double-click on the **Cisco CTL Client** server symbol and follow the installation wizard. Once the process is complete, you should have a Cisco CTL Client icon on your desktop.

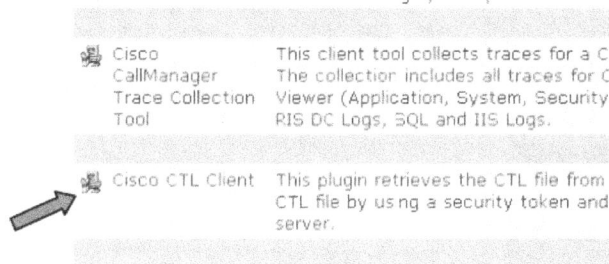

Cisco CallManager Trace Collection Tool	This client tool collects traces for a Cisco CallManager cluster into a single zip file. The collection includes all traces for Cisco CallManager and logs such as Event-Viewer (Application, System, Security), Dr.Watson log, Cisco Update, Prog Logs, RIS DC Logs, SQL and IIS Logs.
Cisco CTL Client	This plugin retrieves the CTL file from the Cisco TFTP server. It digitally signs the CTL file by using a security token and then updates the file on the Cisco TFTP server.
Cisco Customer Directory Configuration Plugin	The Cisco Customer Directory Configuration Plugin guides you through the configuration process for integrating Cisco CallManager with Microsoft Active Directory and Netscape Directory Server.

Step 9. Double-click on the Cisco CTL Client icon to configure your CTL Client.

11

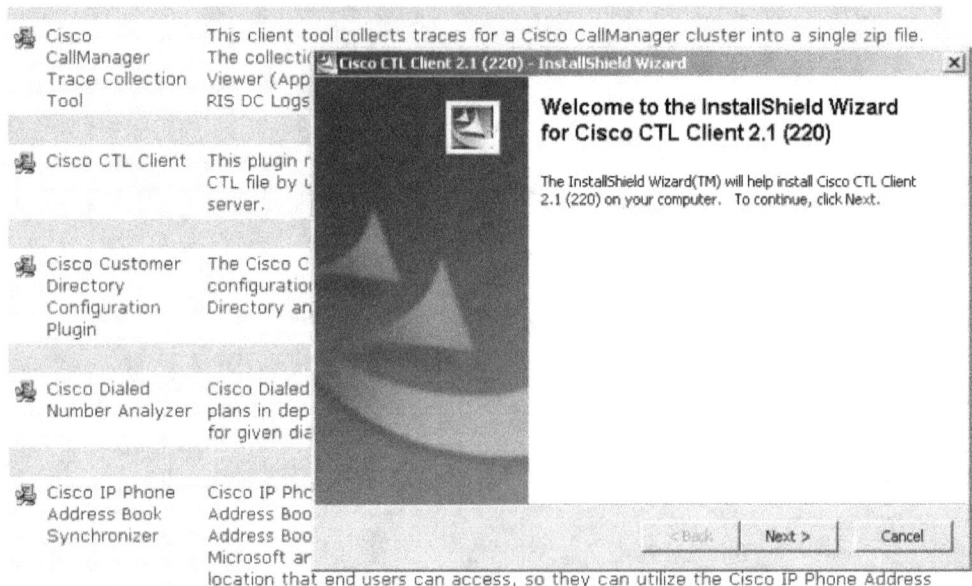

Step 10. In the Hostname or IP Address field, insert the IP address of your CCM.

Step 11. Enter the Username and Password for your CCM and click Next.

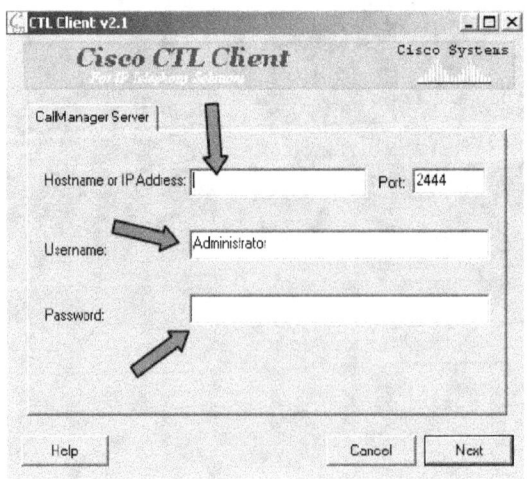

Step 12. Click on **Set CallManager Cluster to Mixed Mode**.

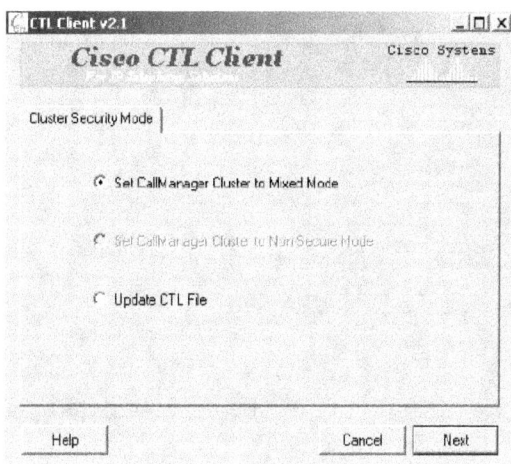

Note: Mixed mode allows authenticated or encrypted Cisco IP Phones and non-authenticated Cisco IP Phones to register with CCM. In this mode, CCM ensures that authenticated or encrypted devices use a secure SCCP port.

Step 13. Insert one Cisco security eToken in an available USB port on the server and click **OK**.

Step 14. The security eToken information displays for the token that you inserted and click **Add.**

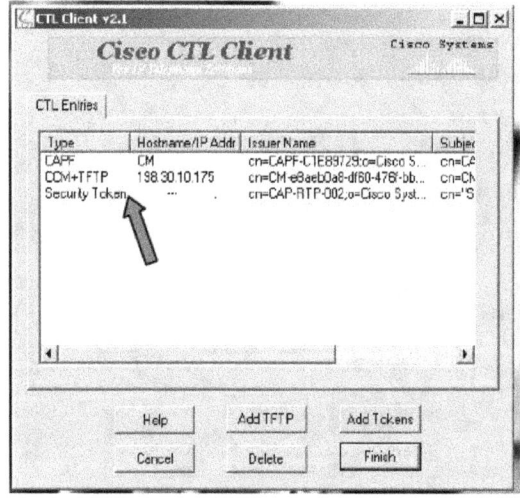

Once the installation of the first security eToken is completed, the token information will be displayed in the Cisco CTL Client screen.

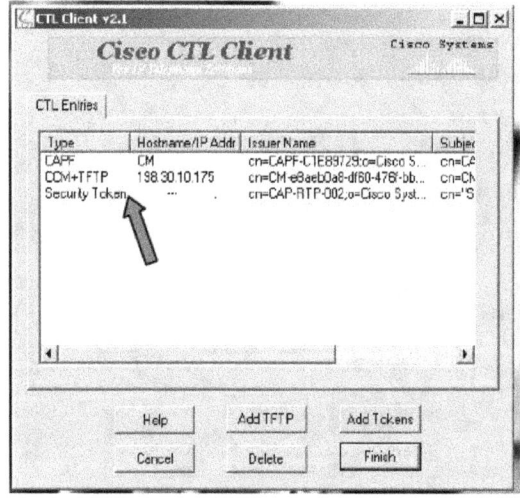

Step 15. You will be prompted to add the second Cisco security eToken using the using the same steps.

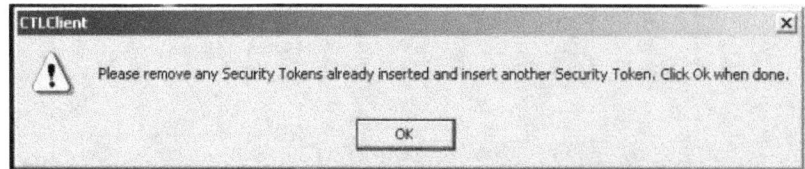

Step 16. If you need to add an alternate TFTP server, click **Add** TFTP Server.

Step 17. When you have added both Cisco security eTokens, click **Finish**.

Step 18. Enter the username password for the Cisco security eToken. The default password for the eToken is **Cisco123.** Be sure to change the default password and take appropriate steps to secure the password. For steps on changing the default password, go to Section 4.3 on page 17.

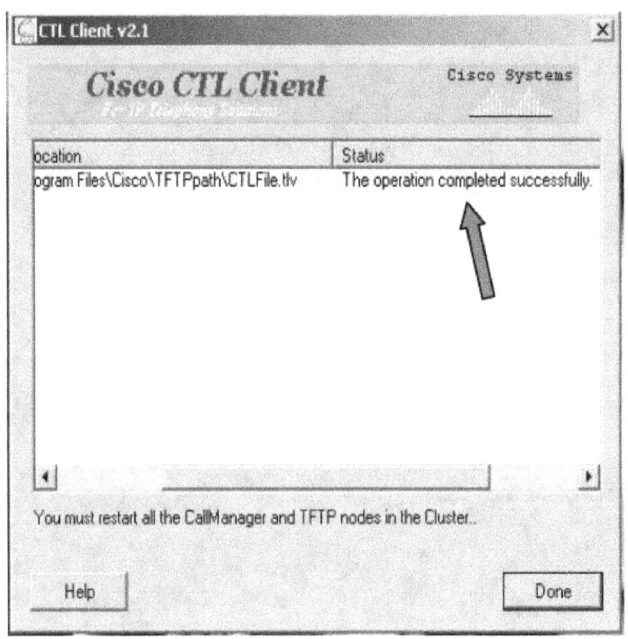

Note: All Cisco security eTokens have a retry counter for the token password. After 15 consecutive "incorrect" attempts, the eToken will be locked and unusable.

Step 19. Click Done.

Step 20. Remove the eToken from USB port.

Step 21. Reset all devices in the cluster by going to Cisco CallManager Administration, choose **System** > **Cisco CallManager** > click on **Reset Devices**.

Note: As stated earlier, configuring security services should be performed during maintenance hours. Resetting devices in step 22 might have an effect on existing sessions.

Step 22. Go to **Cisco CallManager Serviceability** > **Tools** > **Control Center** > restart Cisco CallManager and Cisco TFTP services in each CCM server in the cluster.

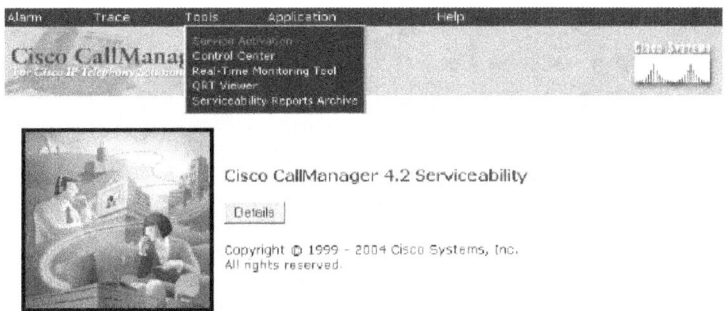

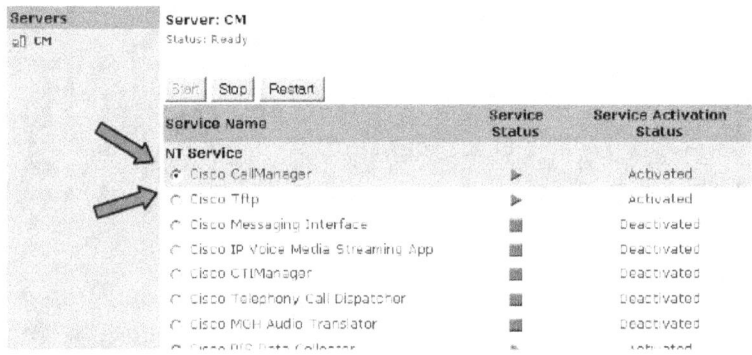

4.3 Changing the Cisco Security eToken Password

Step 1. On the Windows server where your CCM is located, choose **Start → Programs → etoken → Etoken Properties;** right click **etoken** and select **Change etoken password**

Step 2. In the Current Password field, enter **Cisco123** (default password)

Step 3. Enter a new password

Step 4. Re-enter the new password to confirm

Step 5. Click **OK**

5.0 Configuring the Phone for Security Mode

The next step is to configure the phones for security mode. There are three methods to configure the phones for security mode. Those three methods are:

- Configure the system default device security mode for supported phone models.
- Configure the device security mode for a single device.

- Configure the device security mode for a supported phone model by using the Cisco Bulk Administration Tool.

This document provides instructions to set default device security mode and single device methods. Due to the in-depth procedures for using the Bulk Administration Tool method, detail instructions can be obtained in the Bulk Administration Tool User Guide.

When the IP phone is configured for authentication, the service provides integrity and authentication for the phone using TLS connection with NULL/SHA. When the IP phone is configured for encryption, the service provides integrity, authentication, and confidentiality using TLS connection with AES128/SHA.

5.1   System Default Device Security Mode

In Cisco CallManager the setting for the system default device security mode for all phone types is Non-Secure. To change the setting in the enterprise parameters to Authenticated or Encrypted, perform the following steps:

Step 1. From Cisco CallManager Administrator, select **System → Enterprise Parameters.**

Step 2. Scroll down to Security Parameters section and find the **Device Security Mode** field.

Step 3. Click on the drop-down menu of the **Device Security Mode** and select **Authenticated** or **Encrypted.**

Note: Selecting encrypted in this field in CCM will provide both authentication and encryption functionalities. The encrypted option is highly recommended.

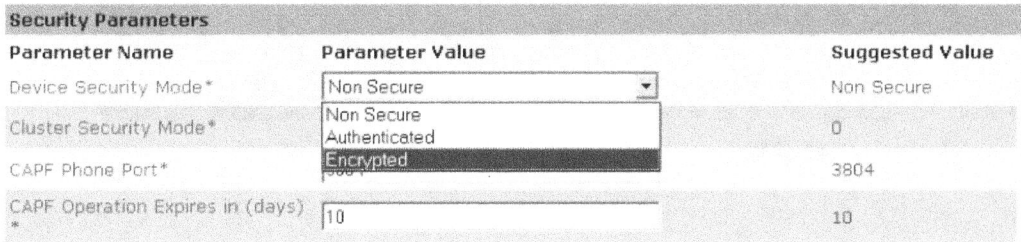

Security Parameters		
Parameter Name	**Parameter Value**	**Suggested Value**
Device Security Mode*	Non Secure ▾	Non Secure
Cluster Security Mode*	Non Secure / Authenticated / Encrypted	0
CAPF Phone Port*		3804
CAPF Operation Expires in (days)*	10	10

Step 4. Go to the top of the screen and click **Update.**

Step 5. Reset all devices in the cluster by going to Cisco CallManager Administration, choose **System** > **Cisco CallManager** > click on **Reset Devices**.

Step 6. Go to Cisco CallManager Serviceability > **Tools** > **Control Center** > to restart Cisco CallManager service.

5.2 Security Mode for a Single Device

Step 1. From Cisco CallManager Administrator, select **Device → Phone.**

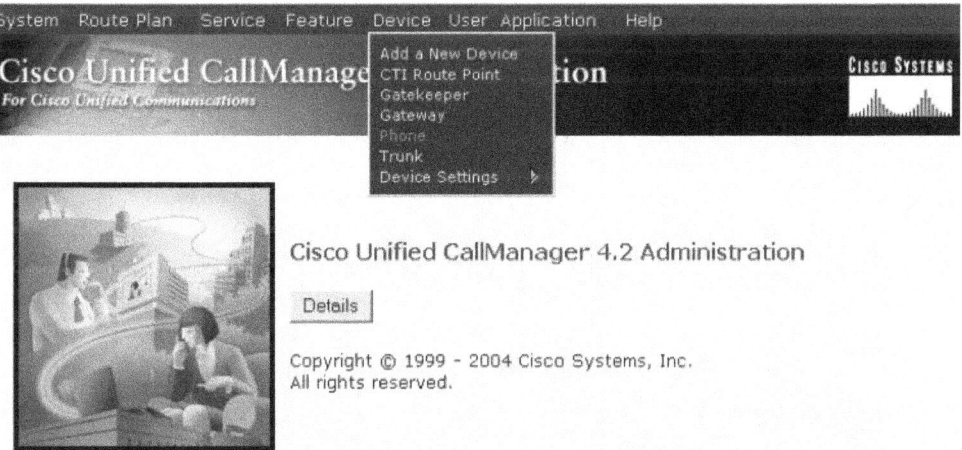

Step 2. Click on **Find** to display the list of all phones.

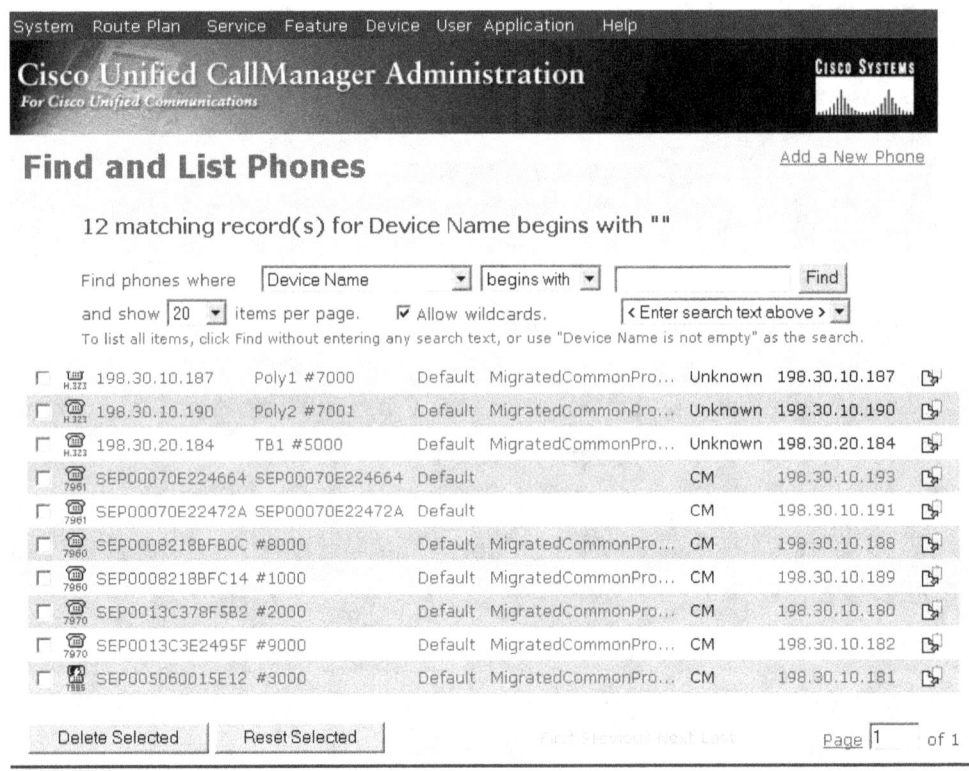

Step 3. Click on the specific phone that you want to configure security and scroll down to locate **Device Security Mode** section.

Step 4. Click on the drop-down menu and select **Authenticated** or **Encrypted.**

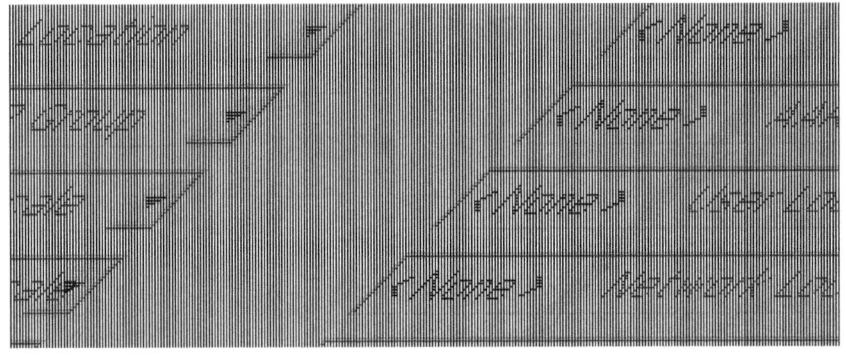

Note: If the phone does not support the security service, the option for selecting security mode will not be available.

The next step is to configure CAPF service on the phone. Go back to *step 1* and *step 2* from above and this time select **Certificate Authority Proxy Function** instead of **Device Security Mode**.

Step 5. At the Certificate Operation field, select **Install/Upgrade** from the drop down menu.

Step 6. At the Authentication Mode field, select **By Existing Certificate (precedence to LSC)** or **By Existing Certificate (precedence to MIC)**, or By **Authentication String** based on what came as the default installation on your devices. The **By Null String** option is not recommended because it provides no security when the phone is attempting to authenticate with CAPF.

Note: The LSC and MIC are certificate authority types. The MIC is a Cisco certificate authority and LSC is a certificate generated by the CAPF or a third-party certificate authority. With certain phone models, a LSC and MIC certificates can exist in the same phone. The LSC takes precedence over the MIC for authentication to the CCM server.

The option of utilizing a third-party certificate authority is available in Cisco CallManagers. Detailed instructions can be obtained in the Cisco CallManager Security Guide under the "Using a Server Authentication Certificate from a Third-Party Certificate Authority" section.

Step 7. Click **Update.**

Step 7. Click **Reset Phone**.

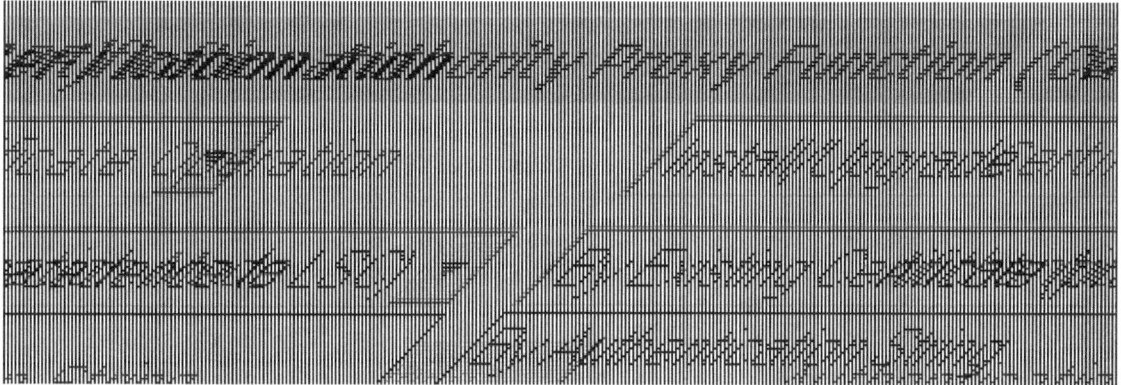

6.0   Hardening the Phone

To further tighten security on the phone, the following settings are recommended:

- Disabling Gratuitous ARP
- Disabling Web Access
- Disabling PC Voice VLAN Access
- Disabling Settings Access
- Disabling PC Port

Disable the Gratuitous Address Resolution Protocol (ARP) - Gratuitous ARP is when the Cisco IP Phone receives an unsolicited ARP reply, that is an ARP reply when the phone did not send a request, then uses this unsolicited ARP reply to update its ARP table. By doing so it is possible to spoof a valid network device. Gratuitous ARP is enabled by default on Cisco IP Phones.

Disable Web Access – When Web Access is disabled, the phone will block HTTP port 80. With this setting disabled, users will not be able to access the phone's internal web pages to view statistic and configuration information.

Disable PC Voice VLAN Access – The default factory setting for Cisco IP phones is to forward all packets that are received from the switch to the PC port. When this setting is set to "disabled" a PC connected to the PC port will not be able to sniff the traffic coming to the phone that is VLAN tagged.

Note: Cisco IP Phone models 7940 and 7960 drop any packets tagged with the voice VLAN. Cisco IP Phone model 7970 drops any packet that contains any 802.1Q tag on any VLAN.

Disable Settings Access – This capability setting provides a user the ability to access information about their phone (e.g., network configuration, user settings, and model information). The three options for this field are Enabled, Disabled, and Restricted. When the "Disabled" option is selected, configuration settings and network information will not be viewable by local users. When the "Restricted" option is selected, only user preferences and volume settings can be modified on the phone display.

Disable PC Port - By default, Cisco CallManager enables the PC port on all Cisco IP phones that have a PC port. A primary example of usage of the PC port from a user perspective is when the user only has one Ethernet drop. A computer can be connected through the IP Phone PC port for connectivity to the network. If this feature is enabled, it becomes even more imperative to have the PC Voice VLAN Access set to disabled.

In general, there are two methods for hardening the phones. The first method is to harden the phone individually. The second method is to create a device pool configuration for the CCM group. This document provides instructions for the individual phone hardening method. Detailed instruction for creating device pool configuration can be found at http://www.cisco.com/en/US/docs/voice_ip_comm/cucm/admin/4_0_1/ccmcfg/b02devpl. html.

To harden the IP phones using the individual phone method, perform the follow the steps:

Step 1. From Cisco CallManager Administrator, select **Device → Phone.**

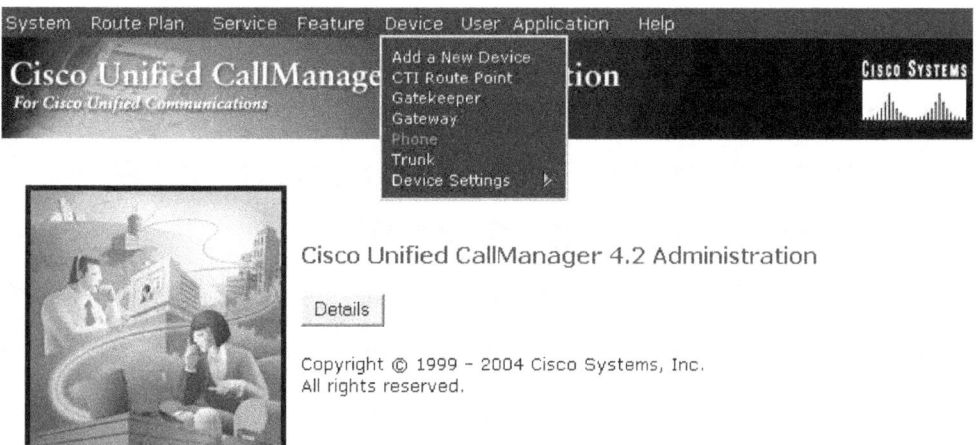

Step 2. Click on **Find** to display the list of all phones.

Step 3. Find the specific phone that you want to harden.

Step 4. Double click on that phone and go all the way to the bottom of the menu to the
Product Specific Configuration.

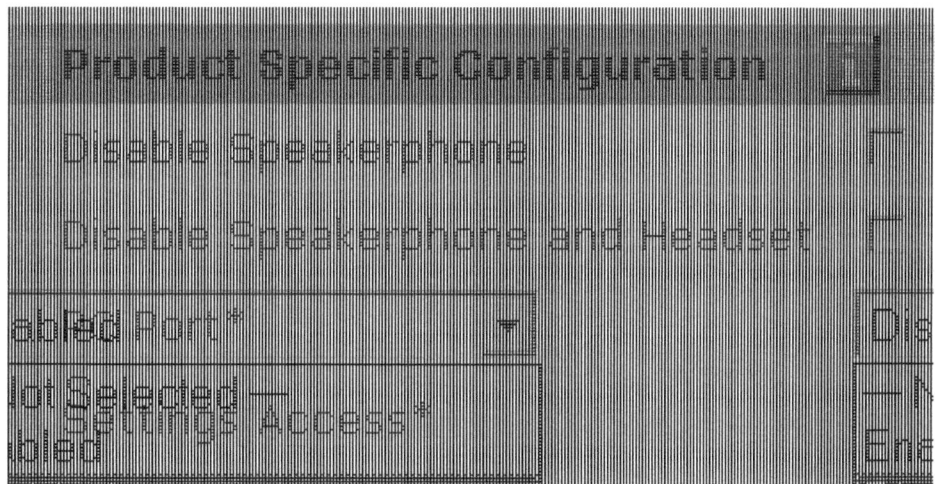

Step 5. Use the drop down menu for each parameter and choose **Disabled**.

Step 6. Click **Update**.

7.0 References

Additional information on this topic can be found in the following documents:

Cisco CallManager Security Guide (Releases 4.0.(x) – 4.3.(x)).
Security Guidance for Deploying IP Telephony Systems
Bulk Administration Tool User Guide.